STOP WAITING TO FEEL READY

The Story You Tell Yourself

Kim Musikant

Cover Illustration By My Niece, Sophia Mohrmann, Who Brought The Image Of A Kintsugi Vase To Life–A Fitting Tribute To A Book About The Beauty Found In What's Been Broken And Repaired.

AUTHOR'S NOTE

I almost didn't write this book. Not because I didn't have anything to say, but because somewhere along the way I convinced myself I wasn't an author. Who am I to write a book? Does anyone even want to hear this? What's so special about my story? This book is what I learned about moving anyway - not once the fear disappeared, but alongside it. If you're standing at your own version of that door - wondering if your story is worth telling - I hope these pages give you a reason to open it.

TO MY FAMILY, FRIENDS, AND CLIENTS

To Marty and our kids. You are my WHY. You are the reason I wake up every day and keep going, even on the days it would be easier not to. Everything I build, I build because of you.

To my family and friends, who have listened to every version of this story long before it had a title, thank you for showing up, again and again, without ever asking me to be anything other than myself.

And to my clients, the ones who let me into their lives, their struggles, and their wins. You taught me as much as I ever taught you. This book is, in many ways, yours too.

Thank you for your support over the years.

TABLE OF CONTENTS

CHAPTER 1

The Slow Fade

I used to be scared of old people. They seemed cranky and unapproachable.

I also grew up hearing the message: Old age is downhill. Old age is loss. There was proof right in front of me too. Whenever I visited my grandparents' house, my grandfather was in the same spot: a green recliner, pulled up close to the TV, which was situated separate from the rest of the living room. When we visited, he didn't say much. He didn't get down on the floor and play with us, didn't ask us questions, or really interact much at all. He'd retired at 65 and just sat in that recliner. That was it. That was what he did with the rest of his life. He watched TV.

The whole house felt old to me back then: outdated and worn furniture, the smell of mothballs, everything a little dim and a little tired. Looking back now, though, my grandparents weren't old at all. They were probably about my age. I didn't know any different. To me, this is how grandparents were. Old wasn't a number . It was a recliner, a quiet house, and a man who'd decided he was finished.

When you see black balloons and "over the hill" signage for birthdays of people over 50 throughout your entire life, the message is clear: old people have nothing left to offer. I grew up thinking that life starts to decline after a certain age. Somewhere along the way, we decided getting older was something to mourn instead of something to earn.

It wasn't until I actually became one of those "old people" myself that I realized how wrong that whole picture had been all along.

I'm not the only one who's figured this out, either. Turns out there's actual research behind it.

Stage, Not Age by Susan Wilner Golden is full of stories of people starting businesses in their 70s, building, not slowing down. Golden's whole argument is that the old three-stage life, learn, earn, retire, doesn't hold up anymore. That was the script my grandfather's generation got handed: retire and go quiet. It's not the script anymore. More than half of America's small business owners today are over 50, and most of them didn't start because they had to. They started because they finally had the freedom to chase something they actually wanted. Businesses started by people in their 50s and 60s survive longer and grow faster than those started by twenty-somethings, not despite their age, but because of it: the experience, the network, and the money already saved up.

The same thing is happening with degrees. People who go back to school after 30 end up earning close to the same as people who did it the traditional way. It's not some symbolic gesture. It actually pays off. An entire generation is quietly doing this now, building and starting over well past the age when their grandparents clocked out, while the birthday cards keep making the same tired joke.

I see it in my own life, too. I went back to school to get my master's at 50, a decision that's really its own story, one I'll get to later in this book. My husband and I are now 59 and 64, and we just finished our second Spartan Race together, hauling ourselves over walls and through mud pits alongside people half our age. Nobody out there was checking birth certificates at the starting line. Age didn't disqualify us from anything. It just meant we'd gotten a little smarter about how we trained for it.

That second race meant something to me for a specific reason: the year before, we'd run our first Spartan Race, which was our 2025 misogi. We first learned about a misogi in our business mastermind group. Here it is in a nutshell: once a year, you take on one challenge so hard there's a real chance you won't finish it. The only rule is that it has to push you, physically and mentally, to what you're actually capable of when there's no easy way out. Also, you can't die.

My 2026 misogi is writing this book, so here we are.

I want to be clear about something: Misogis aren't necessary to age better. This was a personal choice I made, a way to challenge myself, not a requirement or a rule for anyone else. Whether you decide to take one on or not isn't the point. Maybe it inspires you to find your own version of a hard, once-a-year challenge. Maybe it doesn't, and that's fine too. I don't want anyone reading this to feel like they're falling short because they don't have a Spartan Race or a book on their calendar. Aging well doesn't have a required checklist. This is just what it looks like for me.

And a misogi doesn't have to be physical. Mine happened to be, because that's where my own edge lies, but yours doesn't have to look anything like an obstacle course race. It could be reading ten books by the end of the year. It could be finally booking the trip you've talked about for a decade. It could be living somewhere else for a year, just to see who you become in a different life. The form doesn't matter. What matters is picking something that pushes you somewhere you're not sure you'll make it, and refusing to quit halfway through anyway.

Last month, we spent the weekend hiking some steep hills, hanging out with our grown, married children, working out, playing pool and ping-pong, and just keeping up with their level of energy.

This isn't the exception. This is what's possible when you stop believing those dumb balloons.

If aging isn't downhill, what is it?

I think of it as an ever-evolving stage of empowerment.

If you have kids, they are grown. You are no longer spending every ounce of energy keeping small humans alive.

It's a time of reinvention and excitement. You get to be yourself again, except now you're not starting from scratch. You've got decades of wisdom and experience behind you, and the power to build anything you want on top of it. That's not a decline. That's the most exciting position you could possibly be in. So here's your permission slip, if you need one: you're allowed to want more. More adventure, more strength, more reinvention, whatever "more" means for you. You didn't survive the hardest, most exhausting years of your life just to coast quietly into "downhill." You built something.

I want you to ask yourself the following questions: What is my Spartan Race? What is the thing I haven't done yet because I've been telling myself I'm too old, too busy, too whatever, the thing that scares me a little and calls to me anyway? I will give you a hint on how to figure it out: it's already in your heart. You just have to listen.

Life is busy. The demands are real. Most of us are juggling full-time work, caregiving, and endless to-do lists. When time feels scarce, it's easy, understandable, even, to put your own needs last. Taking care of everyone else feels like the responsible thing to do.

But there's a cost to running on empty. Eventually, it catches up with your health, your energy, and your mindset.

That's the slow fade.

Not a dramatic collapse, just quietly putting yourself last, year after year, until "downhill" starts to feel true simply because you stopped showing up for yourself.

Before a plane takes off, the flight attendant always says the same thing: if the oxygen masks drop, put yours on before your child's.

If I were that flight attendant, I would tell everyone why we do that. I would say something along the lines of, "If you pass out, who is going to help your kid?"

We do this to ourselves all the time, sacrificing our own needs for the people we love, thinking that's what devotion looks like. Please do not neglect your own mental and physical health for the sake of others. That makes no sense.

That's the real slow fade, not aging itself, but quietly going unconscious to your own needs while you take care of everyone else's.

So put your mask on first. When you move your body, rest, and nourish yourself, you don't just feel better, you function better. Your energy rises. Your confidence rises. And from that place of strength, you have more to give: to your family, your work, your community, and yourself.

That's not selfish. That's the opposite of the slow fade. That's what it looks like to choose the empowerment stage instead.

Try This: The Mask-On Audit

For one week, before you say yes to something that drains you, ask: Am I putting my mask on, or handing it to someone else? Write down every time you notice yourself defaulting to last.

CHAPTER 2

The Sentence That Carried Me

"For I know the plans I have for you," declares the Lord, "plans to prosper you and not to harm you, plans to give you hope and a future." (Jeremiah 29:11, NIV)

There are two ways to measure where you are in life: against how far you still have to go, or against how far you've come. Most of us default to the first one without ever realizing we have a choice. I did, for years, until I learned I had a choice. I could choose thoughts such as, "I am behind in life," or I could look back and see how far I had come.

Dan Sullivan and Dr. Benjamin Hardy have a name for this in their book The Gap and the Gain. The gap is the distance between where you are and some ideal, always-just-out-of-reach version of your life. The gain is everything you've actually built, measured against where you started. Gap thinking feels like ambition. It isn't. It's a machine for making sure you never feel like enough, no matter what you accomplish.

I didn't have any of this yet at 38. Not the skills, not the language for it, not any of it.

At 38, after eight years of pouring myself into the care and feeding of my children, it was time to return to work after the divorce. Not only did I want out of the house and some adult interaction, but I was ready to go back to work after being a full-time mom. But I was adamant about getting not just any job. I wanted to do some soul-searching to uncover my passion. More than anything, I wanted to be one of those people who jumped out of bed excited to get to work, someone who'd turned a genuine passion into an actual career.

I knew I wasn't going to return to my former career before having children in the "computer industry," as we called it back then. Technology had changed too much over the past ten years. Besides, I wanted a fresh start in something new.

I wanted to explore my options. I was planning it out, being intentional and analytical about it, the way you'd design something custom-made instead of picking something off a rack. I didn't just want a job. I wanted to feel in alignment with whatever came next, something that felt like it was actually me, not something I was settling for because it was available.

So I sat down and made a list of things I loved. Gardening was on it, until I pictured myself in one of those big landscaping trucks doing the physical labor that came with it, and I immediately crossed it off. Not that. Fitness, though, had been part of me for as long as I could remember. That felt true.

By this point, I'd already made the leap, practicing on neighbors in my own basement before I ever taught a real class, getting certified, and working my way from being a group fitness instructor at the Y, where Jean had talked me into teaching my first official class years earlier, to becoming a personal trainer at a gym. I was doing the thing.

I came across an idea during this time of soul-searching to write what is called a Major Definite Purpose. Brian Tracy came up with this term, and here is the definition: A Major Definite Purpose is the one guiding purpose that gives direction to your life. It becomes the filter through which you make decisions, prioritize your time, and stay focused on what matters most.

I was already a trainer, but I was not leaving any stone unturned, so I started writing. I came up with the following as my MDP: To educate, empower, and help people achieve their goals for better health and well-being through lifestyle changes.

This wasn't just idle daydreaming, either. It was a financially desperate time. There was a month when I had to take money out of all three of my children's savings accounts just to pay rent. That's not an exaggeration. I think back and cringe. It was the lowest point of my life. The shame I felt at the bank was awful. It felt like everyone knew what I was doing and was judging me. My landlord knew what I had done. He said, "Thank you for doing that." I don't expect handouts, but I still wonder if that guy felt anything that day.

This was a dark stretch. I remember closing the shades during the day, not because of the sun, but because I didn't want anyone looking in, didn't want anyone seeing how low I'd gotten, or didn't want to be judged for where my life had landed. I was depressed. I was vulnerable in a way I hadn't been before.

My sense of worth back then wasn't coming from anywhere close to the truth. It was coming from a failed marriage, from the word "divorcee," from living in a town where every family I passed looked intact and happy while mine had just come apart. Lots of people told me to stay in the marriage, that the consequences of leaving would be too great.

My argument back then was simple: I want to be happy today. I didn't want to wait to be happy "someday." One friend told me, "Wait until the kids are in college." I remember looking out my window once and seeing the dad next door playing with his kids in the yard, and feeling this wave of sadness wash over me. I had constant pity parties back then, sitting in that same window, watching a life I didn't have.

I measured myself against the gap, the distance between where I was and some imaginary life where the marriage had worked, where I hadn't failed at the one thing I was supposed to protect. I never once measured myself against the gain.

Because the gain was right there, if I'd allowed myself to see it. I had three wonderful children whom I loved immensely. I had a bachelor's degree, I was a personal trainer, and we were all healthy. I had a lot to offer the world, even if I couldn't feel it yet. And underneath all of it, I believed God was going to provide, even when I couldn't see how. That was the gain.

That's when I started praying, reading the Bible, and trusting that Jesus had me covered.

But shame doesn't measure gain. Shame only knows how to measure the gap. I still catch myself in the gap occasionally. My mind starts running ahead with worries like, How will we retire? When? Some of my friends are already retired. Gap thinking, dressed up in a new decade.

The difference now is that I catch it fast. I recognize the shape of it almost as soon as it starts, that old habit of measuring myself against some finish line up ahead instead of against how far I've already come. And when I catch it, I can choose the gain instead: I've been married for eleven years to a man I adore, I have three grown children who are healthy and thriving, we have a business we built from nothing, and a second career, my dream job as a therapist. That's not a gap. That's a gain.

Somewhere in that stretch, I picked up The 7 Habits of Highly Effective People by Stephen Covey, one of a stack of books I was reading while trying to rebuild myself into someone more solid. I felt that if I made myself "better," I would be more valuable in the workplace. And these types of books helped me do that. In this book, Habit 2, "Begin with the End in Mind," affected me greatly. Covey's point is that if you know how you want to be remembered, you can make decisions today that align with that vision.

I sat with that question for a long time, and I still use it to this day. I have also encouraged others to use it. That question said nothing about surviving a divorce, or getting by, or holding it together for the kids. It was something bigger than my circumstances at that moment. I wanted my life to have mattered to people beyond myself and beyond my children. I wanted to leave the world a better place.

It was out of that darkness, the closed shades, the empty savings accounts, and the prayers, that I finally put into words what I'd already been living toward: To educate, empower, and help people achieve their goals for better health and well-being through lifestyle changes.

Looking back now, I think that sentence was as much about fear as it was about purpose. Somewhere underneath the desperation, there was also this quiet terror of disappearing into an unremarkable life, a divorced woman who just got by, with nothing more said about her than that. I didn't have the words for it then. I just knew I needed my life to matter to someone beyond myself, and I wasn't going to wait around to feel ready before I started proving it.

I didn't need the sentence to start the work. I'd already started. But I needed it to keep going, to remind myself, on the darkest days, exactly why I was doing what I was doing.

That sentence shaped everything that came after. It's why I kept training clients through a divorce, through single motherhood, and through starting over. It's why Marty and I opened Active Life Fitness after refusing to sign that non-compete. It's why we rebuilt after the fire. That's why I'm writing this book right now.

I'm still living out that same Major Definite Purpose today, sixteen years later: to educate, empower, and help people achieve their goals for better health and well-being through lifestyle changes. Every client, every class, every page of this book, it all traces back to that sentence I wrote in the middle of the darkest stretch of my life.

One of my greatest fears back then concerned my kids. Not just getting through that stretch, but what it would do to them long-term. I worried deeply about them "turning out okay." I got plenty of judgment for the divorce itself, even from people in my own family, and plenty of quiet opinions about what getting divorced would do to three young kids.

Turns out, all three of my children have grown into mentally and physically healthy adults, thriving in their own careers and relationships. Two are married. My middle child and his wife also have a baby on the way! I don't say this to brag. I say it because I remember exactly how unsure I was that this outcome was even possible.

I think about those mornings often, pulling out of the driveway at 5:45 a.m. to be at my job as a personal trainer by 6:00 a.m., leaving the kids asleep to get themselves up and ready for school on their own. I remember the fear, wondering if something would happen while I wasn't there, a fire or something else, and I wouldn't know until it was too late. Those mornings were some of the hardest of my entire life, not because of any one crisis, but because of the constant low hum of not being sure. Not sure how rent would get paid. Not sure how food would get on the table. Not sure if leaving my kids alone that early was the right call or just the only one I had.

I sometimes wonder what would have happened if I'd stayed in that marriage instead of leaving. I don't know for certain, but knowing what I know now about addiction, about instability, and about what kids absorb from the home they grow up in, I don't think they would have turned out this way. Maybe that's not fair to say. But it's what I believe.

I didn't know it yet, sitting there with the shades closed, but I'd just written the thing that would carry me through everything else.

Try This: Gap Or Gain

Tonight, write down three things about your life right now. Then ask: Am I measuring them against an ideal I haven’t reached, or against where I started? Rewrite each one from the gain.

CHAPTER 3

Be A Honey Badger

I got the house in the divorce settlement. There was close to $200,000 in equity sitting in it, and for a while that felt like something solid to stand on. I should have sold it right away. Instead, I waited, and the 2008 crash hit, and by the time I finally did sell it, it wasn't really a sale so much as a rescue. It went into a short sale, and I had to come up with $5,000 just to get out from under my own house.

I moved into a rental two blocks away, and somehow that turned into one of the unexpected joys of that whole stretch. It had a pool table. It shared one long driveway with three other houses, all of them intersecting at the same spot. There were kids everywhere, riding bikes, skateboards, and throwing a ball around from morning to night. My kids were thrilled. For a minute, it felt like I could actually start over, breathe, and put a little money away.

That's when the real trouble started.

There's a certain kind of person who won't let you fall apart quietly. Gina was like that. We worked together at the gym I'd eventually get fired from. She ran the facility, and I saw her nearly every day, though we were coworkers more than friends. She was matter-of-fact, not warm and fuzzy, all muscle, and she owned two huge Great Danes. I remember being a little miffed at her once when she was trying out all the trainers in the facility to see which one she liked best, and she didn't choose me.

"Don't take it personally," she said. "I prefer male trainers."

That was Gina. Blunt, no cushioning, whether she was picking a trainer or telling me to get my act together.

She caught me at the front desk one day, right by the counter where they made the shakes, and just said it, in front of whoever happened to be standing there:

"Kim, be a honey badger!"

Someone pulled up the video right then and there, and a few of us crowded around and watched it together, laughing, right at the counter. I couldn't stop watching it after that. I must have watched it thirty more times over the next few weeks, and I showed it to everyone, coworkers, clients, anyone who'd sit still for two minutes. This honey badger was hungry, and he was on a vicious mission for his next meal. Bees swarmed and stung him. He kept going. A venomous snake bit him. He passed out cold, and when he woke up, he just kept moving. Nothing stopped him. Nothing slowed him down. Tunnel vision, straight to the goal.

Gina wasn't the type of friend who coddled you and told you everything was going to be all right. She was the type who showed you a video of a rabid honey badger, in front of an audience, and said, essentially, get your shit together. Get tough and suck it up.

I needed that more than I needed comfort. Sympathy would have let me stay where I was. What I actually needed was permission to toughen up and keep moving.

I was going through a hard stretch at the time. Years after my divorce, my ex wasn't reliable, and I never knew whether support would come or not. Some months it did. Most months it didn't. I stopped being able to plan around it at all. A friend who was an accountant helped me make sense of the numbers. A friend who was a lawyer helped me pursue what I was legally owed.

Except, mostly it didn't matter. He was MIA more often than not. The kids had no idea where their father was for stretches at a time. He'd disappear for months, then call out of nowhere, say all was well, and ask to see the kids. Then the cycle would start again. There was a stretch where I told my oldest son he'd need to get a job himself if he wanted new clothes for school. My confidence had taken a beating. People were starting to notice. Gina wasn't having it.

I needed someone steady in the middle of all that, and I found it in a few different places.

One was my friend Brigid, one of the first friends I made when I moved to New Jersey. We ran the NYC Marathon together, raised our kids together, and our boys were all around the same age, playing sports together, with our families going in and out of each other's houses for years. She later became a realtor, so she'd seen every kind of emotional upheaval there is around buying, selling, and renting a home, and she understood exactly what I was going through when I lost mine. She's still one of my best friends to this day, and she was one of the people who quietly pointed me back toward my faith during that stretch.

Another was the owner of the gym, the same one who'd eventually let me go over a non-compete. He became a real mentor to me during that stretch. When I started as a trainer, I was unsure of myself, walking the floor trying to land new clients, not at all confident that I knew what I was doing. Everything changed when he told me a quote from Maya Angelou: "People don't care how much you know until they know how much you care." After that, business started booming for me because caring for people is my specialty. It always has been. I went to him regularly with my problems, more like he was a mentor than a boss. I remember telling him once, crying, not joking at all, "Jesus can't pay my rent." He didn't flinch. He just kept pointing me back to the Bible anyway, patient with me even when I wasn't ready to hear it.

Somewhere in the middle of all of it, on top of a mound of laundry in my basement, I hit a point I couldn't push through anymore. I fell to my knees right there on the floor, crying, and asked God to take over because I could not do this anymore. That was the moment. Right there, on top of a pile of laundry, I decided to allow God to guide my life. I couldn't control what my ex did or didn't pay, whether he showed up or disappeared again. But I could control how I moved through it, and that I didn't have to carry all this alone.

Around that same time, I'd been training a male client for a while, and we'd gotten close. I confided in him about what I was going through, the divorce, the money, all of it. He knew. He never said a word about it, though, not for a long time.

It was only much later that he mentioned that his wife, Meg, ran a nonprofit she'd started herself called Gateway, one that helped divorced and single moms get back on their feet. Not long after that, she started coming into the gym to train with me too, except training was never really the point. Long before she ever helped me with a single bill, she was teaching me the Bible, patiently helping me actually understand it, helping my faith grow from something the size of a mustard seed into something that could bear weight. Eventually, her organization started helping me with my bills. Literally.

The owner had been right all along. Jesus did end up paying my rent. He just took his time getting there.

And somehow, it worked. If a half-blind, venom-immune rodent could get stung, bitten, knocked out cold, and still keep pushing toward what he wanted, what was my excuse?

I was tired of living the way I was living. I was willing to try anything.

Stung, bitten, knocked flat, and still moving toward what I wanted anyway. I learned and tried to practice regularly the following: My past does not define me, and it doesn't define you either. That's what the honey badger was really teaching me: refuse the gap between where you've been and where you're going. It's a mentality I've had to call on more than once since then, whenever life handed me something that should have stopped me cold.

I don't know where Gina is today. She wasn't in my life long, just a coworker who happened to be exactly what I needed for one hard season. Some people aren't meant to stay. They just show up long enough to say the one thing you needed to hear.

Try This: Sort The Wheel

Name one thing right now you can't control, and one thing you can. Hand God the first one, out loud if you have to. Then take the one action inside your control today, regardless of how you feel about the rest.

CHAPTER 4

The Pit Bull And The Pant Leg

Fear doesn't wait for you to be ready, and neither does desire. The two can occupy the same body at the same time, and whichever one gets louder is the one that moves you. Matt Furey writes about this in Theatre of the Mind, building on Dr. Maxwell Maltz's work: desire itself is a force strong enough to carry you forward even while fear is still fully present and hasn't gone anywhere.

I didn't believe that yet the day Jean first asked me to teach. I believed the opposite, that fear had already decided the answer for me.

She came up to me after class one day and asked, "Have you ever thought about teaching?"

"Yes, I have thought about it," I told her. "But it won't happen because I would never get up in front of a group of people." To me, it wasn't an option. It was off the table, and no negotiation or convincing would ever change that. I wasn't wishy-washy about it. I was matter of fact about it. There was no way I was going to get up in front of a bunch of people and teach a fitness class. I wasn't even like, "Oh, that really scares me, so no way." It was an absolute, laughable, "No way, not gonna happen" kind of thing.

It would be nice if I were different, but that was not me.

But Jean, the head of group fitness, was like a pit bull tugging at my pant leg. She was a petite woman, all muscle, and had the biggest, brightest smile you'd ever seen. Jean was a ball of energy, the kind of person everyone in that building loved. When you talked to her, she made you feel like the most important person in the world. She was positive, uplifting, and genuinely funny. She would not let up. Every time I saw her, she'd ask again: "Have you thought any more about teaching?" "You would do so well." "You have perfect form." Every time, I gave her some version of no. Although, I must admit, she did wonders for my ego!

Somewhere in that persistence, maybe it was all those compliments and bright smiles, something started to shift in me. It wasn't that I suddenly stopped being scared. It was that Jean's belief in me became louder than my own doubt. She saw something in me that I couldn't yet see in myself, and eventually, her confidence in me became the confidence I needed to finally say yes.

But it wasn't only Jean's belief carrying me. Somewhere in there, I noticed something shifting in myself too: my desire had become stronger than my fear. This was desire finally outweighing fear, exactly what Furey was talking about.

She changed my life. Not with one grand gesture, but with relentless, patient persistence, the kind that doesn't let you hide behind "that's not me" forever.

So I got certified.

Two hours before my first class, I was curled up on the couch in a fetal position, running through a hundred excuses in my head. I could call Jean and tell her I was sick. I could say one of my kids was sick. I could claim I'd forgotten about another commitment entirely, anything to avoid walking into that room and standing in front of people. But underneath every excuse, I knew the truth: Jean wouldn't believe a single one of them.

The fear wasn't really about the choreography or the moves. It was about being seen. What if they didn't like me? What if my class wasn't good, simply because it was my first one and I didn't know yet what I was doing? That's imposter syndrome in its rawest form, the fear that you're about to be exposed as someone who doesn't actually belong in the room you just walked into.

And underneath even that was my inner critic, a voice that had followed me for years, long before Jean ever tugged at my pant leg: "What do you think? You're a fitness professional now?" I wasn't just fighting my own doubt that day. I was fighting something I'd been carrying for a long time.

But underneath the panic, I knew none of those excuses would help me. If I backed out, I'd feel horrible about myself afterward, worse than any fear I was feeling in that moment. And I'd still have to face this eventually. Canceling wouldn't make the fear disappear. It would just delay it, and delaying it would only make things worse.

So I got off the couch. I got in the car. I drove to the Y, and I taught my first class.

The fear didn't disappear all at once. It faded slowly, class by class, as people kept coming back, as validation started to outweigh the doubt, one returning face at a time.

But here's what I've learned since: That feeling doesn't leave for good. It just goes quiet for a while, until something new wakes it back up. Years later, in the middle of a hard stretch, I remember thinking, "What made me think I could go back to school and get a master's degree at this age?" Same voice, just aimed at a different goal.

Even now, if you asked me to walk onto that gym floor and teach a class of eleven people again, something I haven't done in years, it would terrify me. Not because I don't know how. Because that old fear doesn't check your résumé before it shows up. It doesn't care how many degrees you have, how many classes you've taught, or how many times you've already proven it wrong.

Try This: Do It Scared

Pick the thing you've been telling people "That's not me" about. Set a real date and tell one person who won't let you back out. Show up anyway, scared, unprepared, and imperfect, and let the fear fade after, not before.

CHAPTER 5

Sit Down And Shut Up

That fear never fully leaves, but it doesn't mean it wins. Let me back up to right after that first class at the Y, because that's where the real shift started.

There was no single moment where fear turned into love. It happened gradually. I kept showing up, kept teaching, and each time, it got a little easier. The dread I felt before that first class slowly loosened its grip. Then, one class at a time, something started to shift. This wasn't just something Jean had talked me into anymore. It was becoming mine.

Slowly, three things came together at once: the support of the women in my classes, Jean's steady encouragement, and a growing confidence in myself every time I stood in front of the room.

People kept coming back. Week after week, the same faces showed up, for me. I remember thinking, almost in disbelief, They're coming for me? How is that possible? It was such a foreign feeling that all I could think of was that old Sally Field moment: "You like me! You really like me!"

Except this wasn't an award show. This was real life, and it was happening to me.

That realization gave me something I hadn't felt in a long time: the feeling that I could actually make a difference. That I wasn't just a divorced, broken woman trying to piece her life back together. I had something to offer. Something real. Something people wanted.

That was the beginning of my own why, not Jean's belief in me anymore, but something I was starting to believe in myself.

But believing in myself wasn't something that happened once and then stayed that way. It's never been that simple. Self-doubt doesn't disappear just because you've had one good class, one good year, one moment of feeling like you finally have something to offer. It's ongoing. It's a continuous process, not a single finish line.

Even now, that ugly face of doubt still shows up. It still asks me the same questions it always has: When will I get over this? Aren't I too old for this?

I don't think those questions ever fully go away. I think you just get better at recognizing them for what they are: old, familiar voices, not new evidence that you were wrong about yourself.

There's a name for this kind of thinking. In my clinical work, it's called catastrophizing, jumping straight to the worst version of a story before it even happens. It's one of several unhelpful thinking patterns I teach my clients to watch for, and I ask them to do the same thing I've had to learn to do myself: catch it before you fight it. Notice the thought. Name it. Ask whether it's a fact, or just a familiar old habit wearing a fact's clothing. You don't have to win the argument with that voice right away. You just have to recognize it for what it is before it convinces you it's the truth.

Mind reading is another one I see constantly. I have a client who does this in nearly every conversation with her husband: she imagines exactly how he's going to respond, decides she already knows the answer, and never actually asks him. It shows up across every topic, not just one: money, plans, anything. Over time, it built real anger and resentment because she was making decisions based on an answer he never actually gave her. He wasn't the one shutting her down. Her own imagined version of him was.

We started with a CBT thought record together, writing down the assumption, then testing it against what actually happened when she did ask. I also taught her assertive communication, specifically using "I" statements, so she could say what she needed without either attacking him or disappearing into silence. She's becoming more confident in how she actually feels, and she's doing the real work now: catching the thought before it runs the whole conversation, and using her own voice instead of having a conversation that only ever happened in her head.

I have a hard side. Ask anyone who's known me for a while. When I hear someone drifting through life, unconscious, small, staying in the same cocoon year after year because it's familiar, something in me wants to shake them by the shoulders. Get up. Get your ish together. You have more in you than this.

But here's the part I don't say out loud as often: that voice isn't only aimed outward. It's aimed at me too, probably more than anyone. Every time I've almost let myself go quiet, almost stayed small, almost let a hard season convince me that this was just who I was now, that same hard-ass voice is the one that got me back up. Sit Down and Shut Up wasn't just something I learned to say to doubt. It's something I've had to say to my own cocoon more than once.

And yet. There's another whole side of me that isn't hard at all. With Marty, I get to be the delicate one. The one who needs looking after, who wants comfort and safety and love without having to earn it or prove anything first. That side is just as real as the honey badger. Neither one cancels the other out.

I used to think that was a contradiction I needed to explain away. Now I think it's just what a whole person looks like. Tough enough to drag myself out of my own cocoon. Soft enough to still need someone else's arms once in a while. You don't have to pick one.

A few years ago, Jean stopped by our gym to see me, no warning, no heads up, just showing up one day. I saw her and literally grabbed her, picked her up off the floor, and swung her around in a circle. We both laughed hysterically. She told me how proud of me she was.

Try This: Catch The Voice

Next time doubt shows up, write down the exact sentence it says. Underneath it, write, "Old voice, not new evidence." Keep a tally for a week. You'll likely find it's repeating itself, not telling you anything new.

CHAPTER 6

Three Months' Notice

Marty and I worked for the same gym. He had been there for 14 years, and I had been there for 5 years when the owner presented us with a non-compete. Now? Why now? You do that when you first hire people, not after they have been with you for a while. So, the non-compete basically said that if we left the gym (got fired or quit), we could not do the same work in the following towns, and the document named all the surrounding towns within a 5-mile radius. In my head, I was thinking, "So this document is basically saying to switch fields altogether." It was asking me to rewrite my MDP.

We went back and forth over this non-compete for months, reading, rereading, negotiating, consulting trusted friends, and finally consulting an attorney who basically laughed at it. He said it would never hold up in court.

The owner may have also suspected something was going on, that we had one foot out the door anyway.

I always noticed the hours Marty put into his job, long hours, being trusted, and being loyal to the company. One day, months before any of this, I told him, "You are basically running this business. The hours you work are as if you own this place." I like to think I got in his head a little. He's always been an incredible leader, the kind who can take a brand-new coach and turn them into an excellent trainer. And I knew I brought something different, the vision, the creative side. Between the two of us, we had what it took to build something real. I just didn't know yet if we'd get to choose the timing, or get pushed into it.

So when the non-compete showed up, I stopped waiting to find out. On one of my breaks, I walked over to Santander Bank in Garwood and opened a business checking account. I remember walking back down the street afterward, proud, confident, like I was on a mission. Whatever happened with that non-compete, we were going to have something of our own.

Then it happened.

Marty got called into the owner's office first. I was in a separate office, going about my morning, when the door opened and Marty walked in.

"I just got fired," he said. "And you're next."

I remember sitting there for a minute, having to process it. My first thought was closer to relief than anything else: Cool, we can collect unemployment and take the summer off. Before I could even fully take it in, the owner called me into his office too. Same conversation, same outcome. I was fired, minutes after Marty.

Marty was furious. Fourteen years, that's how long he'd been there. I understood why he was so upset. This felt like a punishment for asking reasonable questions about our own careers after that many years. I'd only been there five. Maybe that's part of why my reaction was different. I wasn't shocked. Some part of me had already made peace with it weeks earlier, sitting in that office waiting my turn, that bank account already open down the street. I just remember thinking, well, there it is. I knew it was coming.

We didn't go to the beach. We got on the phone instead and called every one of our clients to tell them the news. We were shocked by the response. Client after client told us they'd follow us, wherever we landed next. It was humbling in a way I wasn't prepared for, realizing we'd touched enough lives that people wanted to stay with us, not the gym, not the name on the building, us. It reminded me of that same feeling from years earlier at the Y: They like me, they really like me, except this time it wasn't about a fitness class. It was about whether two people could actually build something real together, and apparently, we already had.

We found that "bring your own client" gym, the kind of place that rents you space and lets you build your own book of business inside it, and we started over there. About 75% of our clients followed us. That number still means something to me. It wasn't our job title or the gym's name that kept people coming. It was us.

Those first few weeks felt strange. Some part of me kept waiting to feel free, and instead I just felt punished, like bad karma had caught up with us for something, even though I couldn't have told you what. It faded, but it took a while.

We cut back on a lot that year, following Dave Ramsey's advice almost to the letter, his whole plan, step by step. We'd seen a few other spaces before finding the one that became Active Life Fitness, but we both knew it the moment we walked in.

Honestly, I don't remember a lot of standout moments from that year. It was mostly just the grind, doing what we had to do, day after day, until enough of those ordinary days added up to something real.

I don't remember getting the keys, but I remember the place sitting empty right after everything was delivered and installed, all the equipment finally in, nobody in it yet but us.

The phone wasn't ringing. We argued about why.

"Well, I don't know what to do," Marty said.

"Well, I have no idea what I'm doing either," I told him.

One day, I was on the other side of the gym when I heard a loud bang. I came running to see what happened. Marty was flat on his back on the floor, still on the phone. He'd fallen backward off a stability-ball chair, one I'd bought so the two of us would be sure to engage our cores while we worked. He didn't want to lose the sale he was making, so he just kept talking like nothing had happened, like he wasn't laid out flat on his back on the floor of our own gym. I still think about whether the person on the other end of that line heard the sound. I wonder if it's one of our clients, still with us today.

Try This: What Good Came Out Of It

Think of a setback you're facing right now, a job, a relationship, a place you had to leave. Instead of listing what you lost, write down what it taught you, or what got better because of it.

CHAPTER 7

Motion Creates Emotion

A few years ago, I sat in a large conference room full of fitness industry professionals at a Perform Better seminar, listening to Martin Rooney speak. At some point, he asked the whole room if anyone knew the Rocky theme song. Then he had every single one of us, a room full of trainers, coaches, and gym owners, stand up, jog in place, raise our arms overhead, and sing the theme song from Rocky together.

I sighed, stayed planted in my seat, enjoying my coffee, and said to myself, "I am not doing this ridiculous thing. I came here to sit and listen." After he persisted in asking everyone to stand, and I watched the audience slowly start to get to their feet, I wanted to walk out. "It is way too early for this. I am not interested in this silly game."

But Martin Rooney knows how to get a room moving, and we all did what he said. And that was the whole point of the exercise. Even when you don't feel like doing something, when you take action, the feeling follows. As Tony Robbins puts it, "motion creates emotion."

Nike built an empire on this idea. "Just Do It" was never "just do it if you feel like it." Between 1988 and 1998, that slogan took Nike from $877 million to $9.2 billion in global sales because people didn't wait to feel motivated. They put the sneakers on, and the motivation showed up after.

Looking back on that room, I think about the three things that were probably running through everyone's heads when Rooney asked us to stand up and sing:

First, maybe you don't think you have it in you. I still deal with this. As a business owner, I struggle with self-doubt regularly. If you do too, act first. Let the motion create the emotion.

Second, maybe you just don't feel like it. How many times have you said, "I don't feel like going to the gym. I'll go later," only to find that later never came? I see this with clients all the time. They arrive tired, not wanting to be there. Halfway through the workout, they're energized. Motion creates emotion.

Third, maybe it's fear. A few years ago, at our gym's grand opening, my husband Marty asked me, "Will you be saying a few words tonight, sweetheart?" My heart started pounding. My palms got sweaty. I froze and said no, I hadn't prepared; it was too late. I was petrified of public speaking, frozen at the mere thought of it.

But here I am now, still in motion. Still doing the very thing that used to paralyze me.

There will always be things we don't want to do that we have to do. We're wired to gravitate toward what feels good and avoid what feels hard. But the things that feel hard are usually the things that push us just past our comfort zone, and that's exactly where the breakthroughs happen.

This book is the latest proof of that, for me. I avoided writing it for a while. I told myself I couldn't focus, that I had too many distractions, that I needed the right conditions before I could really sit down and do it.

Someone planted the seed years before I ever started. I met Thomas Plummer in 2020. Within seconds of meeting him, he looked me square in the eyes and simply said, "You should be speaking and writing." I think I said something like, "You don't even know me." But I never forgot it.

Years later, at Plummer's Speaker School, I asked him if he remembered the first time we met. He went quiet. Everyone else at our table went quiet too. He said yes, but his body language told a different story. Based on the reaction at that table, I clearly had him stumped. I called him out on it right there. Turns out, he had no memory of ever saying it to me at all.

After Speaker School, we've kept in touch, and I plan on going again in the spring.

It was Vince, the leader of our business mastermind group, who pushed me to actually set a deadline for the book. I went to a branding workshop he ran back in the spring, and for those of us who wanted to write a book, he made us set a deadline.

Yesterday, I organized my house, just enough to take a deep breath and feel a bit lighter. This morning, my head felt a little lighter as well. So today, I sat down to write.

"I need to clear my house first" was never really about the house. It was waiting to feel ready. It was perfectionism wearing a disguise, and its friend, imposter syndrome.

Who am I to write a book? I'm not a professional writer. I don't have an English degree. I've never published anything before. What makes me think anyone wants to read a book that I wrote?

I recognized the voice immediately, though, because I'd heard it before. It's the same voice that told me I'd never get up in front of a room and teach a fitness class. The same one that told me I was too old to go back to school for my master's. Different goal, same script, right on schedule, exactly like it always is.

And I already know what to do with that voice, because I've done it before.

Sit down. Shut up.

You don't run this.

Then I write anyway, the same way I kept teaching anyway, the same way I went back to school anyway. The voice never actually leaves. You just get faster at recognizing it for what it is.

The next time you don't feel like doing something—writing the book, going to the gym, giving the speech, having the conversation—think of that Rocky song. Start with motion. The emotion will follow.

Try This: The Five-Minute Rule

Whenever you're stuck, commit to five minutes of the physical motion involved to move forward, not evaluating how you feel first. At the five-minute mark, decide whether to keep going. Most of the time, the motion will have already made the decision for you.

CHAPTER 8

A Certain Age

One of the core values at our gym, Active Life Fitness, is "Better than yesterday." The books that I reference throughout this book are some of the ways I have kept getting better and committed to being a lifelong learner.

I want to share an exercise that was eye-opening for me after I read Stephen Covey's The 7 Habits of Highly Effective People. It's called "Begin with the End in Mind." Here's how it goes: picture your own funeral. What do you want people to say about you at the end of your life? How will your eulogy sound?

That exercise had a profound impact on me. It made me realize that I don't want to have an ordinary or mediocre life.

I didn't expect to be reminded of that answer in a hair salon waiting room. But that's exactly what happened.

I was sitting in the waiting room at the hair salon, minding my own business, when I overheard two women who looked like they were in their late fifties talking about a "certain age" like it was a life sentence. Doom and gloom. The kind of negative self-talk that just accepts things as they are now, like there's nothing left to do about it.

I sat there biting my tongue. Closing my eyes, hoping it would stop. Telling myself, Do not interact with them. I should have gotten up. Gone to the bathroom. Grabbed a coffee. Put myself literally anywhere else in that salon.

At the gym, my clients know that if I hear this kind of talk, I'm most likely going to deliver my "we become what we think about most" speech, how negativity leads us down the path of self-fulfilling prophecies. So when I heard it in that waiting room, my heart started beating a little faster, and my face felt hot. I kept my head down in my magazine, trying to mind my own business, hoping they'd change the subject.

They didn't. They kept going, talking about how difficult life is at their age, how their bodies are no longer the same.

Then, I heard myself say, "It doesn't have to be that way. I know lots of people your age who feel great. It's all about lifestyle choices."

By the time those words left my mouth, my heart was pounding so hard I was sure they could hear it too. That's usually how it goes for me right before I say something I know I probably shouldn't. The moment right before is always the worst part, the debate happening in my own head, the part of me insisting I mind my business fighting the part of me that simply couldn't sit there another second.

It just came out.

There. I said it. It was a weak moment for me, but I want everyone to feel their best and live a long, healthy, active, pain-free life, physically and emotionally. I'm just living by the Major Definite Purpose I wrote back in 2010.

Here's the point: if we think life is all downhill once we reach a certain age, that's exactly what we'll get, a tired, achy, blah existence. If we think about how beautifully we were created, and choose to nourish our bodies with real food, movement, and rest, we get more of that instead. Our bodies thank us for it.

I don't remember if they said anything back to me. But, if my memory serves me correctly, I think they ignored me. Looking back, I would have ignored a person who interjected his or her opinions into a private conversation I was having with a friend too. But I was tired of it. Tired of people who complained and did nothing about their self-proclaimed miserable existence.

Walking out of that salon, I felt two things at once, and neither one canceled the other out. I felt proud of myself for finally saying something I actually believed, instead of just biting my tongue and stewing about it in my head the way I usually do. But I also felt a little embarrassed, replaying it in my mind, wondering if I'd overstepped, if I'd come across as preachy or self-righteous to two strangers who hadn't asked for my opinion in the first place. Both feelings were true. I didn't need to pick one.

I don't know exactly what it was about those two women that got under my skin so fast. Maybe it was the tone, the way they talked about their lives like a done deal, like the story was already written and there was nothing left to do but complain about the ending. It wasn't really about them, though, if I'm honest. It was about me. It was fear.

Back during one of the hardest stretches of my life, I read every self-help book I could get my hands on, trying to rebuild myself into someone more valuable, more solid, someone who wouldn't fall apart again. That funeral question is the one that never left me.

I remember sitting with that question and feeling restless. I didn't want to be known only in relation to other people, somebody's mom, somebody's wife. Those are a big part of who I am, for sure, but I wanted more. I wanted my life to make an impact on the world beyond my own four walls. Something bigger. Not because a smaller life is any less meaningful for someone else, but because it wasn't true to what I actually wanted for my one life.

That's the fear underneath the anger, if I'm being honest. Those two women in the salon weren't the enemy. They were a mirror, a glimpse of the ending I've spent decades actively fighting against. Every time I see it in someone else, some small, resigned, story-already-written version of a life, it doesn't just annoy me. It terrifies me. Because some part of me is always checking: is that me? Could that still be me if I stop pushing?

It won't be. Not because I'm better than anyone. Because I decided a long time ago exactly what I wanted said at the end, and I've been building toward it ever since.

"Extraordinary" is not about being famous, or admired, or having strangers recognize me somewhere. It is always about impact. About whether my life actually changed anything for the people in it. That's the same thing I put into words back when I wrote my Major Definite Purpose, to educate, empower, and help people achieve their goals for better health and well-being through lifestyle changes, except that sentence came out of me during the darkest stretch of my life, and this fear showed up decades later, in a hair salon, on an otherwise ordinary day. Same fear. Same fire underneath it. It never really left. It just waits for the right moment to remind me it's still there.

Try This: Begin With The End

Do the exercise for real. Picture your funeral. Write down exactly what you want said about you. Then write one sentence about whether today's choices are actually building toward that, or away from it.

CHAPTER 9

Not An Option (Or: Dissing God)

"There's a cop at the door."

I turned over in bed to find my husband looking out the window. My heart sank, adrenaline flooding my body. Before I could even remember if any of our teenage children had gone out that night, I was already up the stairs doing a headcount. Everyone was home. I knew I could handle whatever came next.

We went downstairs and opened the door.

"Do you own a business on South Avenue in Garwood?" the officer asked.

"Yes," Marty answered.

"There's an active fire in the area."

We were in the car within minutes. When we got there, a woman with a calm smile offered us coffee. I couldn't even answer her. I just turned to Marty and asked if we were dreaming.

The fire had started next door, in the restaurant, and spread into our gym. When we were finally allowed inside, the front door was smashed to pieces. The ceiling tiles Marty had installed himself, the ones we'd fought over matching perfectly, were destroyed. Water covered the floors. Holes in the walls. Insulation and glass everywhere. Active Life Fitness, our dream, three months old, was in ruins.

At some point that morning, we texted the kids to let them know about the fire. Our oldest, living at home at the time while he attended a local college, must have gotten in his car the second he read it because, not long after, he pulled into the gym parking lot. He rolled down his window and just looked at us. Shock all over his face.

I walked over to him. He asked me how we were going to pay for things.

I told him we had insurance, that we had business interruption insurance specifically, that we would be fine. I comforted him, told him we'd rebuild, told him it would all be okay. And it was true. We did have insurance. We were fine.

But I understood exactly where that question came from. This was the same kid who'd already lived through the divorce years earlier, who was old enough back then to understand what financial struggle looked like in our house, old enough to feel it, not just hear about it secondhand. He'd already been through more than a kid his age should have to go through once. And here it was again, a different disaster, the same old fear surfacing on his face in a gym parking lot.

I could reassure him about the insurance. I couldn't undo what he'd already learned too early, that things can fall apart fast, and that money trouble is the kind of trouble that reaches everyone in a family, not just the adults trying to fix it.

After the fire, there was never a conversation about whether we'd rebuild. Not one. It simply wasn't a question either of us asked because it wasn't a decision to make. It was already decided, the same way "not an option" had already decided exercise for me. Some things you don't debate. You just do them.

Right after the fire, one of our clients told us about a friend of hers, a woman in her building who needed help. The extra income was welcome at exactly the right time, so I said yes. I started training Sunny in her home, bringing my own equipment since she barely needed any. She was ninety, on oxygen, and used a walker.

It didn't take long to figure out she was seriously wealthy. Her husband had passed away years earlier, but the two of them had built a business together restoring old cars, fancy, high-end ones. She also had a caregiver, and over time, I got to know her too.

When I told Sunny the story of the fire, she looked at me and asked, "Why didn't you just take the money and run?"

It was a fair question. We could have. Insurance money, a clean exit, no more risk, no more debt, no more sleepless nights over a business that had already tried to burn down once.

But I told her the truth: we were devoted to our life's calling. This wasn't just a business. It was the thing we were built to do. And when something is truly your calling, walking away from it is never actually an option, even when every practical voice in the room might have told us it should be.

I believe when something tugs at your heart day after day, a pull you can't quite shake, a nudge that won't leave you alone, that's not just ambition. That's God talking to you. Psalm 37:4 puts it plainly: delight yourself in the Lord, and he will give you the desires of your heart, not despite that pull, but through it. And dismissing that calling isn't just playing it safe. It's dissing God.

I don't remember exactly how it came up, but Sunny's caregiver told me once that her real purpose in the work she did was bringing people to Jesus before they passed, so they could go to heaven. I was still early in my own faith journey at the time, so I was delighted and encouraged to hear this. And she succeeded. Before Sunny passed away, the caregiver told me that she had given her life to Christ.

Sunny taught me not to take life too seriously. Things don't stay the way they are forever. Life is meant to be cherished and enjoyed.

When I found out she'd died, I was devastated. She was so much fun, and so witty, sharp all the way to the end. I went to her funeral. That was it.

So when people ask why we didn't take the insurance money and walk away, the real answer is simple: you don't get to negotiate with your calling. You don't get to wait until it's convenient, or until you feel fully ready, or until the risk feels smaller. You just answer it.

Try This: Name The Non-Negotiable

Identify the thing that keeps tugging at you, the one you keep calling impractical. Write it down as a calling, not a hobby. Decide today, on paper, whether it's "not an option," the same way exercise stopped being optional for me.

CHAPTER 10

Staring Through Empty Windows

The rebuild was grueling. There was no quick fix, no fast reopening. In the meantime, we went back to running a "bring your own client" gym at a local gym, the very same one we'd landed at after getting fired, a year earlier. Same temporary home, twice, both times while we rebuilt something of our own. Ironically, the owner of that gym was a firefighter. We called him the morning of the fire to ask if we could come back, and he already knew about it before we even said a word.

During that stretch, I remember hauling equipment back and forth, trying to recreate our group training atmosphere (our new business model, not the one-on-one setup we'd had before) in a gym that wasn't even ours. The day-to-day was physically exhausting. I remember thinking, more than once, "I am too old for this."

But I kept showing up anyway. Because "too old for this" was just another voice trying to talk me out of my calling, and I already knew better than to negotiate with that.

He strung us along for months, saying he'd fix things, he'd do things, and then doing nothing. Eventually, we brought in a lawyer to go over the lease, and it turned out we had good cause to break it.

By that point, I was worn out from the search. Marty wanted to keep looking at new spaces, so I told him to go ahead without me. When he found somewhere he liked, I'd go see it. That's exactly what happened. He found it. I went and saw it. That's where we are now. This September, we'll celebrate ten years there.

Walking into the space for the first time, I remember worn-out wicker chairs sitting in the waiting area, and bamboo roll-up shades hanging crooked over what turned out to be beautiful windows underneath. The shades came down first, before almost anything else. But even with all of that, the space itself was bright and open, and we could see the vision immediately.

It had actually been a yoga studio for years before it sat empty. I'd taken a class there once, a long time before any of this, taught by the owner, who had a French accent so thick I didn't understand a single word she said during the entire class. Now it was going to be ours.

A few years into that new location, the gym wasn't where it needed to be financially, and keeping it alive meant making a very difficult decision: we had to sell our house.

It wasn't just any house. It was the first house we bought together as a couple, the one we got married in. Marty and I had each already survived a divorce before we found each other, both of us renting separate places, both of us slowly rebuilding something stable after everything had fallen apart once already. That house was proof we'd made it through. Proof we'd built something real together.

Before we even had the keys, we used to drive over just to walk our dog in the neighborhood. I'd stand outside and look through the window, imagining what life would be like living there.

Once we lived there, I had my coffee on that front porch every morning the weather would allow it. Just me, my coffee, and that feeling of quiet, settled peace.

On moving day, the house was empty again. I was alone. I locked the back door for the very last time, and before I walked away, I stared through that same window, the one I used to imagine our whole life through before we even had the keys. Now it was empty in a completely different way.

I remember thinking, When will my day come? When will I ever get ahead? It felt like money had been tight for as long as I could remember.

Going back to a big gym with lots of other trainers ended up being kind of fun, actually. I hadn't realized how much I missed the banter of having coworkers around, since it had just been me and Marty running every session together for so long.

Even the rental we moved into turned out to be more spacious and updated than the house we'd sold. That surprised me. It was fun, in its own way. All of it was, really. An adventure, even the parts that hurt.

Going back to renting felt like losing all over again. I remember being angry, not at Marty, not really at anyone specific, just angry that here we were again, in a financial struggle, after we'd already fought so hard to get past the last one. For a long time back then, life just felt like one long struggle, one setback rolling into the next with barely any room to catch our breath in between.

But we did it anyway. We sold the house that meant everything to us, because the business meant more. Selling the business was not even an option. Not after the fire. And not now, even with a house on the line.

Ten years of showing up, every single day, in a place that almost didn't exist. Ten years that started with a phone call in the middle of the night and a decision that was never really a decision at all, because rebuilding was never a question. It just was.

Try This: The Same Window

Think of a struggle you're in the middle of right now (hopefully, you’re not). Picture yourself looking back at it from ten years ahead, the way you'd look through a window you used to stand at hoping for something different. Write down what you think you'll see.

CHAPTER 11

Just Look Into It

Nineteen years ago, it was the NYC Marathon I couldn't stop thinking about. This time, it was going back to school to become a therapist. People ask mountain climbers why they wanted to climb, and the answer is usually some version of George Mallory's famous reply: "Because it's there." Meaning that there doesn't have to be a reason. That's what this felt like. The nagging, tugging feeling wasn't optional. It wasn't going away. The voice just kept getting louder.

Looking back, that marathon was one of the hardest things I'd ever done. This pull felt exactly the same way, with that same nagging feeling that wouldn't leave me alone until I did something about it.

I'd always wanted to be a therapist, but I'd tucked that desire away while I was raising my kids. I knew, somewhere in the back of my mind, that "someday" it would happen.

I shared this desire with my husband while we were out on a walk in the park.

"Did you know I always wanted to be a therapist?"

"I've always wanted to get my master's in social work."

I was just opening up, confiding in him, sharing a desire I'd never really said out loud before. I even told him about the memory of applying to a social work program "back in the day," when the applications were physical pieces of paper. I remember the thick manila envelope I held onto, but never submitted.

He smiled, validated my feelings, and simply said, "Look into it."

Something about those three words gave me instant relief. Look into it. Not commit. Not sign up. Not figure out the whole plan right then and there. Just... look into it.

Okay, I will do that. I will check out some schools and read about what is involved. I don't have to commit to anything yet. I don't have to make any major life decisions. So I turned to him and said, "Okay. I will."

"Look into it" helped me take this big, potential decision, and make it small and manageable. It took the pressure off and created space in my mind to take a tiny step. Just like the workout that wasn't up for negotiation, this wasn't a decision I had to keep making over and over. I'd already made it, once, and every day after that was just one more step. I used the same trick that got me through hard workouts: don't look at the whole road, the degree, the license, the years ahead. Just look into it. One step.

A few days later, he asked me how the research into the schools was going. I told him the deadline for applying was in two weeks, and that I was seriously thinking about applying. He said, "Go for it."

So I did. A few weeks after that, I got my first rejection letter. I took it personally. I was pissed. The "I'm not good enough," "I'm too old," and "who am I kidding?" thoughts entered my mind. I fought them off, and kept pressing on.

The second school gave me a hard time. They kept coming back to my transcript, asking questions, hesitating. So I kept calling. Again and again, I made my case: I wasn't some kid testing the waters. I was a serious, grown adult who knew exactly what she wanted and was more than capable of doing the work.

Eventually, they said yes.

In September of 2018, I found myself sitting in a class of students half my age and studying next to my three children, who were in college at the same time. The four of us, in school. It felt fun to commiserate with my kids about boring professors, difficult work, and stressful deadlines, but I was loving every second of it. The challenge, learning new material and technology, clearing out the cobwebs in my brain, and, at times, being overwhelmed by the work, research papers, and deadlines. I was their mom, and in a way, their classmate too.

In most of my own classes, I was the oldest person in the room, sitting among students in their twenties, decades younger than me, working toward the same degree.

Balancing it all was brutal. On top of classes, I had to complete unpaid internships, which meant living two completely different realities at the same time. At the gym, I was the owner. At my internship, I was a little nothing, at the very bottom. No title, no authority, no paycheck. Starting from scratch and having to prove myself all over again.

But I kept going anyway, because none of that mattered to me. It was about the calling, being tuned into the desires of my heart.

I got my MSW from Fordham University. That was only the beginning. Next came the LSW exam, then eventually the 3,000 clinical hours I needed, done at a mental health clinic and a private practice, before the LCSW exam itself, the clinical license that actually lets you practice independently.

In January of 2026, I applied cold to a PMAD center at Barnabas Health, for perinatal mood and anxiety disorders, and everything about it seemed to line up. I get to play a mom role to these new mothers, which feels like exactly where I'm supposed to be.

"Look into it." Those three words can take a big decision and make it small and manageable. Sometimes we look at something big as insurmountable. We see the whole picture and decide, "That's too hard." But sometimes you just need to put one foot in front of the other, put the blinders on, and embrace the journey. The journey is where you grow. The journey is who you become while you're doing the thing. It's the person you have to become in order to reach the goal in the first place.

Try This: Just Look into It

Pick the big thing you've been avoiding. Give yourself permission to only research it this week, nothing more. Write down three small facts you learn. That's the whole assignment.

CHAPTER 12

Building The Plane While Flying It

We didn't see it coming, not really, not the scale of it. But when it started to feel close, we leaned on the people we trusted. Vince, the leader of our mastermind group, told us he was getting ahead of it, closing his own gym for two weeks before anyone forced his hand. We trusted him. We'd built that kind of relationship with him over time, the kind where if he moved, you moved too. So we followed suit.

Marty and I wrote an email. We recorded a video on our back deck, the two of us telling our members what we were doing, that we'd be closing for two weeks, "until everything calms down." We had no idea yet how much wasn't going to calm down.

We started running live Facebook sessions for our clients, figuring it out in real time. Then the government shut everyone down officially, and there was no more "getting ahead of it." We were just in it. So we sprang into action. We loaned out every piece of equipment in that gym that wasn't bolted to the floor. Marty personally hand-delivered weights, medicine balls, kettlebells, and steps to members' houses who didn't have equipment of their own.

It felt good, even in the middle of all the uncertainty. It showed our members how much we cared, not just about keeping the business alive, but about their health, their consistency, and the thing we'd built our whole purpose around. Meanwhile, liquor stores stayed open the entire time as "essential," and gyms were shut down completely. The irony of that was almost laughable, if it hadn't been so infuriating. The one thing that actually builds people up, that keeps them strong, healthy, and resilient, got labeled non-essential. We weren't going to let a label stop us from taking care of our people anyway.

We learned how to use StreamYard because we had to, and we went all in, one hundred percent, with no idea whether any of it would work.

In the middle of all of it, we applied for PPP funding to make sure our staff could still get paid. It meant pulling together all of our financials and submitting everything for review. Marty remembers it feeling like a sure bet, that of course we'd get it. The paperwork was in order, and the need was obvious. But even a sure bet doesn't feel certain when everything else around you is falling apart. The application itself wasn't the hard part. The waiting was. Everything back then was an unknown: how long this would last, whether the funding would come through in time, and whether there'd be a business left to reopen once it did.

Through all of it, we tried to model the same leadership Vince had modeled for us: steady, honest, moving forward even without certainty. And our members responded. About half of them kept paying their monthly membership through the shutdown, not because they had to, but because they wanted to help keep us in business. That kind of loyalty is not something you forget.

Here's the part that still stings a little: the month right before the pandemic hit was our best revenue month we'd ever had. And once we reopened, it took two full years to climb back to those same numbers.

It was all we talked about back then. We'd take turns worrying and consoling each other, one of us falling apart while the other one held steady. Early in our relationship, we'd established a rule: when one of us is falling apart, the other one can't. During the shutdown, that rule got tested every single day. When we both landed on worried at the same time, that's when things actually got stressful. But mostly it wasn't like that. Mostly it was Marty telling me we'd get through this, building me back up, and me doing the same for him when it was his turn to need it. There was no fighting, no blame, just the two of us taking shifts holding the other one together.

I remember exactly when the phrase "building the plane while you're flying it" landed for me, really landed, not just as something I'd heard once. I was in one of my live MSW classes at the time, going through all of this with the gym while also trying to keep up with school. In the middle of that class, I shut my camera off because I was sitting there crying, overwhelmed by everything happening all at once.

It wasn't just fear about the virus, or even fear about the business. It was the gym itself, our only source of income, the thing on the line. And some older, deeper part of me recognized the shape of that fear immediately because I'd felt it before. Getting let go from a job for refusing to sign a non-compete. The literal fire that gutted Active Life Fitness three months after we opened it. Now this. Three different times, three completely different circumstances, and the same terrifying feeling underneath all of them: the ground I'd worked so hard to build was about to disappear again, and there was nothing I could do to stop it.

That's when my professor said it: building the plane while you're flying it, and something about hearing it right then, camera off, tears on my face, made it land differently than if I'd just read it somewhere. That was exactly what we were doing. No blueprint. No certainty. Just building it as we flew it, in real time, the same way we'd done after the fire, the same way I'd done after losing that job. It wasn't the first time I'd had to rebuild something out of thin air. It was just the first time I fully understood that rebuilding was simply something I knew how to do.

Try This: The Next Bolt

Name the situation you're in right now with no blueprint. Don't write the whole plan. Write the one next action you can take today.

CHAPTER 13

The Officiant's Camera

My son got married in Medellin, Colombia, in May. It wasn't just a single ceremony; it was five days of events and excursions, a whole group of us doing things together, eating together, dancing together. My daughter-in-law had planned every bit of it herself, not just the wedding, but also the excursions for all the guests, transportation, places to visit, sights to see, meals to eat, every detail already ironed out before any of us landed. Medellin itself felt like jungle meets city: warm people, incredible food, music everywhere, and this kind of energy you don't get back home.

This was the same son who, years earlier, pulled into the gym parking lot the morning of the fire, terrified, asking me how we were going to pay for things. The same one I once told he'd need to get a job himself if he wanted new clothes for school, back during one of our hardest financial stretches. The same one who was still living at home, commuting to a local college. That college is where he met her, the woman he was now marrying in Medellin. I couldn't help but think about all of it, watching him at his own wedding, remembering the scared kid in that parking lot, the kid who once had to work for his own school clothes, now grown, running his own successful business, building his own life on the other side of everything our family had been through.

My daughter-in-law kept telling me, throughout those five days, that people were asking her if I was a model. I laughed it off. I was just the groom's mother, there to celebrate, trying not to cry through the ceremony.

Before the service, while we were all waiting for the bride, the officiant came over to me and told me I was the most beautiful woman she had ever seen. After the ceremony, she asked if she could take a photo of me.

I figured she probably wasn't used to seeing a lot of white women, and I'd had my hair and makeup done professionally for the wedding, which helps tremendously. Colombian women are some of the most beautiful in the world; I didn't hold a candle to them. I figured it was more that I was different from what she was used to seeing. I was flattered, but it didn't occur to me to make anything of it. It wasn't my day. My daughter-in-law was the bride, the main character, and that's exactly where my mind was too.

I didn't think much more about it once we got home. It wasn't some life-changing epiphany. It was just a strange, flattering moment from a beautiful trip.

Then, in June, barely a month later, I was scrolling through Instagram, and an ad stopped me: models over 50. Which, honestly, is proof your phone is listening to you, because I hadn't searched anything like that, hadn't told anyone I was thinking about it, and there it was anyway. I applied immediately. Then I told Marty.

He wasn't surprised in the slightest. He's used to me doing spontaneous, slightly crazy things by now, so it was less "Are you sure about this?" and more "Good for you!" That's one of the things I love about him. He doesn't need to understand the whole plan before he supports it.

I went in for my initial photo shoot, purchased the package, and started applying for modeling jobs on the sites the agency recommended to me.

I arrived at the shoot nervous. Between each outfit change, I sat in the chair for hair and makeup, and I loved every second of it. It felt like being a princess. There were four looks: jeans and a white T-shirt, a workout outfit, something in "my own style," and finally, a gown.

During the actual shoot, the photographer kept guiding me, but I felt stiff as a board the whole time. It was uncomfortable, being looked at and directed like that.

Then we went outside for a street shot. Strangers walked past us, and not one of them knew I wasn't "the real deal." They probably assumed I was an actual model.

Afterward, when they showed me the gown shot, I was shocked. I stared at it for a second, not fully believing that was me.

After the shoot, I pulled the photographer aside and asked her quietly, "Do you think I have a shot at this?"

She went silent for a second. Then she shook her head no.

I wasn't about to let one person's opinion decide anything for me. But I won't pretend that didn't sting a little. She was the photographer. If anyone in that room knew what the industry was actually looking for, it was her.

I kept applying anyway.

I'm still building it. There's no tidy ending here yet, no big campaign to point to, no moment where it all clicked into place. Just applications going out, some answered, most not, the way it goes when you're starting something new at any age. But I keep applying anyway, because "still building it" beats "never started it," every single time.

That's the whole story, honestly. Not a grand reinvention I'd been secretly planning. A wedding in a beautiful place, a comment I laughed off, a suspiciously well-timed Instagram ad a month later, a photographer who didn't believe in me, a husband who said, "Good for you," instead of asking why, and me, still in the middle of it, still applying, still going.

Try This: Do the Thing Anyway

Think of something you've been holding off on until you feel "ready enough," starting a project, reaching out to someone, trying the new thing. Do the smallest real version of it this week, no waiting for confidence to show up first. Then keep going regardless of how it's received.

CHAPTER 14

The Chips N Salsa Test

Willpower isn't a character trait you either have or don't. It's a resource, one you can run out of, the same way you run out of energy or patience, and knowing that changes everything about how you use it.

I didn't understand that yet the afternoon I sat in front of a basket of chips and salsa, starving, determined to prove something to myself.

I was starving. Painfully hungry.

And there they were, the warm, thin, and crispy, perfectly salted chips sitting in a basket with a side of salsa calling my name. But I was trying to "be good" and decided to test myself. Chips and salsa are, without question, harder for me to resist than a bread basket. So I figured, let's see what happens if I just... don't touch them. An experiment, if you will.

The first few minutes were the hardest. I didn't know what to do with my hands. I kept waiting for my husband to notice how challenging it was for me, and was hoping he'd join my plight, have a little sympathy, and maybe ask the server to take the basket away. He didn't. He just kept reaching in, dipping, crunching, clearly enjoying every single chip while I sat there, starving, gripping my water glass like it owed me something.

I was almost mad at him. Not because he was doing anything wrong, just because he got to enjoy them, and I didn't. I distracted myself with conversation instead. I never touched them. Not one chip.

This was a few years back, at a restaurant right next door to the gym, over lunch. It's the crunch that gets me, and the contrast against the salsa. Something about hand-to-mouth eating just satisfies me in a way that bread and butter never does.

Marty knew exactly what I was doing that day. He's always let me be me, and I let him be him, the same way Cat Stevens sings it in "If You Want to Sing Out, Sing Out." That's just how we've always worked.

That's not just a matter of being "strong" or "good." Yes, it's a "muscle" we must use, but it's also a resource we can harness anytime and anywhere we want.

By the time most of us sit down to dinner, we've already made thousands of decisions. Research out of Cornell puts the number at around 35,000 choices a day, and more than 200 of those are about food and drink alone, most of them so automatic we don't even register them as decisions. What to wear, what to say in that email, how to handle a client, a coworker, a kid's meltdown, a doctor's appointment, a grocery list. Every single one of those pulls from the same tank.

In my experience, with clients and in my own life, willpower runs lowest at the exact same time every day: right after work, when the day is finally winding down and it's time to relax. That's precisely when the wine gets poured, the chips come out, the "I deserve this" voice gets loudest. Not because you're weak, because you're depleted. Eating becomes the reward, the release, the stress valve after a day of nonstop decision-making.

I hear a version of this constantly from clients: "I'm good all day, but nighttime comes and I snack all night." That's not a coincidence, and it's not a character flaw. It's the same depleted tank, just showing up after the sun goes down instead of at lunch.

That's what was happening to me that afternoon at lunch, even though I didn't fully understand it at the time. My willpower wasn't a character flaw waiting to be exposed by a basket of chips. It was a resource.

For me, exercise isn't a decision I make each day; it's just not an option to skip. It's not something I negotiate with myself about, the way I might negotiate with a basket of chips. There's no "should I go today?" There's no willpower spent deciding, because I removed the decision a long time ago.

That's why I never experience what so many people describe, losing momentum, falling off, having to "get back into it" after a break. There is no break. There's no gap where motivation has to reappear before I show up again. The workout isn't waiting for me to feel like it. It's just what happens, the same way work happens, the same way picking up my kids happened when they were young. Non-negotiable.

My most successful clients over the years learned to just show up. Day by day, doing the right thing in front of them, not worrying about anything past that.

I used to use the blinders myself before I ever taught them to clients. I found them years earlier, picking my kids up from grammar school. I carried a lot of shame back then, and I taught myself to block everyone out, other parents, their questions, their looks, by imagining blinders on my own eyes, like a horse wearing them. It sees the path directly in front of it, one step at a time, nothing else. That's what I needed to survive pickup time some days. Later, I gave the same tool to my clients. Stop looking down the road at the big picture, the twenty pounds, the finish line, the version of yourself you're trying to become. Just concentrate on the one small step right in front of you today.

There's a scripture I've leaned on my whole life for this exact thing, Proverbs 3:5-6: "Trust in the Lord with all your heart and lean not on your own understanding; in all your ways submit to him, and he will make your paths straight." I didn't have to see the whole road. I just had to trust the one who did, and take the step in front of me.

James Clear writes about this in Atomic Habits, that lasting change rarely comes from willpower or motivation in the moment. It comes from building systems, from making the good choice the easiest one to reach for, so you're not relying on discipline to win a fight over and over again. The blinders were my version of that. Not "resist the chips forever," but "just get through today's workout, today's meal, today's one decision." The system was the blinders. The willpower barely had to show up at all.

Try This: Pick Your Not-an-Option

Choose one decision currently draining your willpower because it's still up for debate. Decide it, once, ahead of time. Write it down as a rule, not a goal: "Not an option," not "I'll try."

CHAPTER 15

The Force Field

I had a client with a dream of becoming a makeup artist—her own business, her own clients, her own brand. Her family had opinions about that, dressed up as love and concern.

I told her to imagine a force field around herself. Not a wall, not something that shuts people out completely, just a force field, the kind where other people's opinions can hit it and simply bounce off without penetrating. They can say what they want. It doesn't have to land. It doesn't have to become hers just because someone said it with confidence, or love, or worry in their voice. Because that's really what I see so often, in clients and in myself: people putting far too much weight on what others think they should do with their one life.

Here's the part I made sure she really understood: most of that advice isn't actually about her. It's about their own comfort level. When you change, when you grow, when you take a risk they'd never take themselves, it makes people around you uncomfortable because your movement asks a quiet question of them too: "Why aren't you doing that?" It's easier for them to hand you a reason to stay where you are than to sit with that question. That's not always malicious. Sometimes it's genuine fear for you. But either way, it's information about them, not a verdict on your dream.

But she'd already jumped ahead to the LLC paperwork, to quitting her full-time job, to the whole leap all at once. Meanwhile, the actual next step sitting right in front of her was so much smaller: film one tutorial video and post it. Build a little credibility. Maybe take on one client. That's it. That's the whole first step. It reminded me of my own "look into it" moment, all those years ago. The big decision isn't actually one decision. It's a hundred tiny ones, and you only ever have to do the next one. She didn't need an LLC to post a makeup tutorial. She didn't need to quit her job to take on one client. She just needed to stop looking at the whole road and take the one step directly in front of her. The blinders aren't about lowering the dream. They're about making the first step small enough that you'll actually take it.

The trap I saw most often, the thing that undid so much good progress, wasn't a bad weekend. It was what people told themselves after the bad weekend. "I was bad over the weekend, so I ruined it." "I can never keep the weight off." That's not information. That's all-or-nothing thinking, one of the most common unhelpful thinking patterns, and it does more damage than the weekend ever could. One setback becomes proof of total failure, and total failure feels like permission to quit entirely.

I've seen this pattern up close in my therapy work too, not around food, but the same exact trap. I have a client who came to me highly anxious, the kind of anxious where her mind would race straight to the worst possible outcome before anything had even happened. A missed text meant something was wrong. A minor mistake at work meant she was about to be fired. That's catastrophizing in its purest form, and it was running her life.

The first step, like always, was just catching it. I taught her to notice the moment her mind jumped to the worst-case scenario, to name it right as it was happening instead of getting swept into it. And she did. She got good at catching herself, faster and faster each time.

But catching the thought was only half the work. Once she could see the pattern, we built on it. I had her practice generating a replacement thought each time and, just as important, giving that replacement thought equal weight with the catastrophic one. Not replacing panic with forced positivity, but genuinely holding both possibilities as equally likely: maybe this is a disaster, and maybe it's actually fine. That's balanced thinking, treating the calm possibility as seriously as the anxious one instead of always handing the anxious one the microphone.

Over time, something shifted. Her anxiety didn't disappear completely; it rarely does, for anyone, but it reduced dramatically. She wasn't living inside the worst-case scenario anymore. She'd learned how to catch the spiral before it started and hand herself another option instead.

But two bad meals aren't a ruined week. A ruined week isn't a ruined year. The horse with blinders doesn't stop and reevaluate its entire journey because of one rough patch of road. It just puts the next foot down. That's all any of us really have to do: not fix the whole picture, just take the next step and let the picture take care of itself.

That's the real power of deciding something is "not an option" ahead of time: it doesn't drain your willpower because there's no decision left to make. The fight is over before it starts.

So here's a question worth sitting with: What's one thing in your life that keeps draining your willpower because you keep leaving it up for debate?

Maybe it's exercise. Maybe it's the wine after dinner, or the scroll through your phone at midnight, or the thing you keep telling yourself you'll start "when things calm down." Whatever it is, the fix isn't more willpower. It's removing the decision entirely—deciding, once, ahead of time, that it's simply not an option. Not today. Not "we'll see." Not an option.

You don't need more discipline. You need fewer decisions standing between you and the life you're trying to build.

Try This: Build Your Force Field

Think of one opinion about your life you've been treating as true just because someone said it with confidence. Picture it bouncing off a force field instead of landing.

CHAPTER 16

There Is No Finish Line

These days, when I'm not at the gym, with clients, or working as an LCSW therapist at Barnabas Health's PMAD Center 20 hours a week, I do lifestyle and commercial modeling as a fun hobby. Anything can happen there. Right now, older models are a hot commodity. Think about the commercials and ads you see on a regular basis—they're all ages, all shapes and sizes. Agencies are looking for real-life people who actually look like that. It's so fun being on set and meeting new people. I've met some amazing people I still keep in touch with. It's a whole other side of me I never knew was there.

There's a commencement speech by Jim Carrey I think about often. His whole message was that your job isn't to figure out how something is going to happen, just to open the door in your own head. Then, when a real door opens in front of you, walk through it. Don't worry if you miss your cue, because more doors keep opening. That's exactly what modeling has been for me. A door I didn't plan for, but that opened anyway. I walked through it. It's given me a level of self-confidence I didn't have before and, honestly, needed.

I was born with a crossed eye. I had surgery to correct it when I was five, but it didn't hold. Slowly, over the years, my eye drifted right back to where it wanted to be, up and in. So I grew up, and then lived most of my adult life, believing that was the thing people saw before they saw anything else about me. Three weeks before Marty and I got married in 2015, I had surgery again. This time it worked. It was life-changing; not an exaggeration. I stopped hating what I saw in the mirror. I stopped wondering where people were actually looking when they talked to me. I must have thanked that surgeon twenty-five times, told him over and over what he'd done for me. I don't think I would have ever gone back to school for my master's if I hadn't had that surgery first. I needed to believe I could be seen before I could put myself in a room to be evaluated by anyone, in any capacity.

So when I started modeling at 57, it wasn't the same fight it would have been years earlier. The eye wasn't the obstacle anymore. But putting my face in front of a camera, at my age, in an industry built for twenty-five-year-olds, still meant choosing myself instead of waiting to be chosen. "Who does she think she is, putting her face out there like that?" That was my own inner critic talking, imagining what other people were probably thinking. And they probably were thinking it. But I get to define me. Not my past. And certainly not them.

"They didn't like you. You're just starting out, so naturally you're going to suck at this. That brand didn't like your content. They're not going to want you for repeat business."

Same doubt. Different decade, different skill, different stage of life. It doesn't matter how many classes I've taught, how many degrees I have, how many businesses I've built, or how many times I've already proven that voice wrong. It still shows up, right on schedule, every time I try something new.

When that voice shows up now, I talk to it the way I'd talk to a bratty little kid throwing a tantrum: "Sit down. Shut up. You don't run this."

And then I keep going anyway.

Life is meant to be seized, not just survived.

Not politely tapped. Not cautiously approached once you feel ready, once the conditions are perfect, once fear finally quiets down. Seized. Firmly. Even while your hands are shaking.

The two women at that salon weren't wrong that life changes as you get older. It does. But they were wrong about what that change has to mean. It doesn't have to mean shrinking. It doesn't have to mean deciding you're finished. It can mean exactly the opposite: that you keep reaching for the next door, the next "look into it," the next thing that scares you a little and calls to you anyway.

That fear I felt in the salon, the one underneath the anger, has been quietly running underneath this entire book since a sentence I wrote in the middle of my darkest year. I don't think it's actually supposed to leave. It's the same fire that got me back up like a honey badger, stung and bitten and still moving. The same fire behind "Sit down and shut up," every time doubt showed back up in a new outfit. The same fire in "Look into it," in "Not an option," and in "Motion creates emotion." It's what got me through the fire that actually destroyed our gym, through the divorce and the years after it, through building the plane while flying it, through going back to school in my fifties, through choosing myself in front of a camera when I finally believed I could be seen. Not fear of dying. Fear of never having mattered while I was here.

So whatever your version of that door is—the book you haven't started, the career you've been circling for years, the version of yourself you've been putting off becoming—stop waiting to feel ready.

You never will. Not really. Not fully.

Feel the fear. Seize it anyway.

And go.

Try This: The One Door

Name the door you've been circling. Write today's date next to it. Commit to opening it this week, scared hands and all.

www.ingramcontent.com/pod-product-compliance
Lightning Source LLC
LaVergne TN
LVHW021132300926
849160LV00010B/976